IN THE
NATIONAL INTEREST

General Sir John Monash once exhorted a graduating class to 'equip yourself for life, not solely for your own benefit but for the benefit of the whole community'. At the university established in his name, we repeat this statement to our own graduating classes, to acknowledge how important it is that common or public good flows from education.

Universities spread and build on the knowledge they acquire through scholarship in many ways, well beyond the transmission of this learning through their education. It is a necessary part of a university's role to debate its findings, not only with other researchers and scholars, but also with the broader community in which it resides.

Publishing for the benefit of society is an important part of a university's commitment to free intellectual inquiry. A university provides civil space for such inquiry by its scholars, as well as for investigations by public intellectuals and expert practitioners.

This series, In the National Interest, embodies Monash University's mission to extend knowledge and encourage informed debate about matters of great significance to Australia's future.

Professor Margaret Gardner AC
President and Vice-Chancellor,
Monash University

KEVIN RUDD
THE CASE
FOR COURAGE

MONASH
UNIVERSITY
PUBLISHING

Monash University Publishing
Matheson Library Annexe
40 Exhibition Walk
Monash University
Clayton, Victoria 3800, Australia
https://publishing.monash.edu

Monash University Publishing brings to the world publications which advance the best traditions of humane and enlightened thought.

ISBN: 9781922464156 (paperback)
ISBN: 9781922464170 (ebook)

Series: In the National Interest
Editor: Louise Adler
Project manager & copyeditor: Paul Smitz
Designer: Peter Long
Typesetter: Cannon Typesetting
Proofreader: Gillian Armitage
Printed in Australia by Ligare Book Printers

A catalogue record for this book is available from the National Library of Australia.

THE CASE FOR COURAGE

Over much of the last decade, Australia's democracy has been slowly sliding into disrepair and despair. Our major national policy challenges go unaddressed. Our economic future is increasingly uncertain. And the country is becoming palpably more corrupt as we drift down Transparency International's Corruption Perceptions Index. It's tempting, but distracting, to point to the usual list of reasons offered by the Australian commentariat for our democratic demise. These include the declining calibre of the political class, the growing polarisation of politics between the far right and the far left (both of whom are populist but neither of whom have an interest in real policy solutions), and the Balkanisation of the political debate into a thousand pieces through the social media revolution and the algorithmic manipulations of Google and Facebook. But this avoids the elephant in the national living room—the uncomfortable truth that stares us in the face each day when we pick up the morning newspaper or turn on the radio, but which, for reasons of personal self-preservation, we have always been reluctant to address. And that is the cancer on our democracy that is the Murdoch media monopoly.

Rupert Murdoch has long abandoned any pretence of running an independent news organisation. He has fully embraced his new operational role as an effective Coalition partner of the Liberal Party, as his editors push the nation further and further to the far right—for example, on climate change. The net result is that there is no longer anything approaching a level playing field in Australian politics. Anyone who doubts this should reflect on the fact that, since 2010 alone, Murdoch through his daily papers has campaigned viciously against the Labor Party in nineteen out of the last nineteen federal and state elections. Murdoch manipulates our democracy in multiple, sometimes crude and occasionally subtle ways. His near-monopoly in every state except Western

Australia sets the tone and parameters for the political debate which, in turn, bleeds into radio, television and social media. Very few of his print platforms are profitable. He holds them for the primary purpose of political power, an ideological influence on policy and the protection of his wider business interests. In Queensland, which now determines the outcome of all federal elections, Murdoch owns virtually all of the state's daily newspapers, which he maintains regardless of their ability to turn a profit. In Australian media politics, Murdoch's power is near-complete.

Murdoch now acts as a protection racket for the Liberal and National parties, providing little accountability on Coalition corruption, incompetence or just plain policy failure. By contrast, his papers run a rolling demolition derby against Labor governments and oppositions, with the single objective of delegitimising their leaders, policies and performance. At a deeper level, together with the Liberal Party, Murdoch works overtime in cultivating a climate of national anxiety, fear and anger through sustained campaigns on deficit, debt and the threat to Australia from ever-changing, but always nefarious, foreign interests. His mission is to create an overall atmosphere of an anxious

Australia that will always be predisposed towards opting for the psychological comfort of sustaining the conservatives in power, because to do otherwise would involve unsustainable economic and security 'risks' for the country. Murdoch having tilled the soil, his conservative Coalition partners, now including Clive Palmer, chime in with forensically targeted negative advertising campaigns, driven by the latest findings from Republican political neuroscientists in America, and aimed at heightening these anxiety levels should people ever be tempted to vote for a political alternative. And the result? The great, silent but side-splitting joke, shared only behind closed doors between Murdoch and his politically compliant Liberal Party sycophants, is their consistent ability to intimidate a majority of Australians into voting against their own interests and values because they have simply become too frightened to consider the possibility of change.

One of the central arguments of this book is that, until the Labor Party and the national electorate have the courage to deal with this underlying cancer on our democracy, we are unlikely to ever see another sustained progressive government in Canberra.

The Murdoch media project is intergenerational. Lachlan Murdoch is every bit as ruthless in the manipulation of conservative politics through the family media monopoly as his father. So unless the Murdochs are stopped, there will never be a level playing field in the Australian media. And there will never be a platform that enables a different political narrative or policy strategy for the nation's future to be properly debated—as opposed to being opportunistically denigrated the moment it emerges.

Taking on Murdoch is hard. People are frightened of his empire because of the damage he can do to a person's or an institution's reputation. Murdoch and his editors behave like swaggering bullies, threatening anybody who stands up to them. Very few people will privately disagree with this diagnosis of the Murdoch problem. But most want to scurry away, or even worse, in some cases negotiate their own private protection 'arrangements' with the Murdoch syndicate, simply in order to be left alone—so long, of course, as part of the greater Faustian bargain, Murdoch too is left alone. Most of what's left of the rest of the Australian media has also chosen to look the other way for fear, too, that they will be attacked, or in the case of working journalists that they will be blackballed from future work in an otherwise shrinking national media market. The nation, therefore, urgently requires a royal commission into Murdoch's abuse of media power to make recommendations on the proper preservation of a contestable media diversity for the healthy functioning of our future democracy. The Labor Party can no longer sit on the sidelines of this debate. It must act. But so too must millions of concerned Australian citizens, as they have already begun to do, by petitioning those in power for a properly empowered royal commissioner to be appointed. It's time—in fact, it's well past time—that we stand up against the bullyboys who run the Murdoch empire, and against the Murdochs themselves. For once a bully is finally confronted, we often find that their much-vaunted and much-feared power begins to crumble.

Once this is done, there are, however, three more things that must change if the Labor Party is to be returned to office—and, more importantly, remain in office over a number of terms in order to bring about lasting reforms.

Labor must demolish the conservatives' political marketing project in its entirety, given that the conservatives, since the COVID-19 crisis began, have repudiated virtually everything they claim to have once stood for—by embracing the twin conservative evils of big government and a deeply interventionist state. This is despite the Liberals having campaigned for more than a decade against fiscal stimulus, debt and deficit as essential policy instruments for dealing with major economic crises. They claimed our global financial crisis (GFC) borrowings were unsustainable. But as of 2020, the Liberals' balance sheets showed five times Labor's net debt and seven times its budget deficit, while still failing to avoid a devastating national recession. However, the collapse of the Liberals' ideological project goes beyond debt and deficit. Despite undermining the longstanding institutional reform and funding of our national health and aged-care system over the last seven years, the Liberals have finally discovered that, in the absence of the public hospital system, we would have been left utterly naked in the face of the coronavirus pandemic. And despite all of the Liberal Party's assurances that they hadn't destroyed Labor's National Broadband Network (NBN) by substituting twentieth-century copper cable for twenty-first-century fibre, the truth is now out: they did destroy the NBN, wasted billions, and left the Australian economy and workforce unprepared for the rigours of working from home with super-slow broadband. In other words, the entire conservative project has been stripped bare. The emperor has no clothes. And it's not a pretty sight. And while the marketing men of the Liberal Party may seek to use the COVID-19 crisis to try to reinvent themselves as 'Labor-Lite', the immediate task for Labor is to lay bare the utterly bankrupt nature of the Liberals' entire economic creed, once and for all. At the same time, however, Labor must also make crystal clear that the Liberals will continue to rip and tear at the country's social and environmental fabric as soon as the political opportunities re-emerge. We will see this across wages and conditions, superannuation, health, education, aged care and climate change.

The Labor Party must also put forward a clear policy vision on the five mega-challenges that threaten our nation's future: reinventing the future drivers of national economic growth by getting ahead of the great technological disruption that is already undermining both our foreign competitiveness and domestic employment; helping working families remain financially afloat during a time of continuing economic crisis and heightening inequality; developing an intelligent, principled and balanced China strategy as Beijing up-ends the global economic and strategic order; leading national and international action on climate change to avoid the long-term devastation of sustained droughts, floods and other extreme weather events; and preparing effectively for recurring global pandemics into the future. The Liberal Party at its core does not believe in planning at this scale. They are ideologically resistant, politically uninterested, and above all intellectually bone-lazy. It is not their reason for being in politics or government. Their interest instead is 'being there' and to enjoy the individual fruits of office, often corruptly. That is their history. That is also their future. Unless Labor governments rise to the national challenge, as we did in national leadership during World War I, World War II and the GFC, history demonstrates that Australia falters.

Finally, Labor must broaden its political base. The shifting structure of the Australian economy demands it, as does long-term demographic transformation and changing societal beliefs. Full- or part-time wage and salary earners now equal eleven million people, or 65 per cent of the voting population. Small business make up another two million voters and 13 per cent of voters. Five per cent of voters comprise full-time students, while 16 per cent are made up of self-funded retirees or pensioners. The mathematics dictates that the Labor Party must become the natural party of small business, independent contractors and sole traders. Furthermore, the longstanding political conservatism of older Australians (despite Labor being the authors, and most generous funders, of the current superannuation and age pension systems) means that the party must secure more political support from those in the pre-retirement age brackets—as well as neutralise fear campaigns on the structure of retirement income. And Labor must become more culturally accommodating of those who continue to hold a religious faith, not just those who don't.

All four tasks—tackling the Murdoch media; rendering the fundamentals of the Liberal project null and void; presenting a coherent, progressive vision for the nation's future; and broadening Labor's political base—are essential. All four require great political courage to bring about lasting change. Otherwise, we should all look forward to life in permanent opposition as the nation slowly drifts into long-term decline. Courage, however, is a strange thing. Courage is not a feeling. If it was, I have to confess there are very few times in my life that I have actually felt courageous before taking a particular course of action. No, courage is simply a decision to act.

MURDOCH, THE LIBERAL PARTY AND THE POLITICAL SCIENCE OF ANXIETY, FEAR AND ANGER

The core reason for this little book is that, for the first time in my life, I have become worried, deeply worried, about Australia's future. I worry because we are becoming a nation riven by anxiety, fear and anger—at times bordering on uncontrollable rage. These are deeply disabling emotions that crowd out the space in our nation's mind and imagination for mostly anything else. They overwhelm our natural sense of optimism, enterprise and generosity of spirit, transforming us instead into a frightened and fractured people—a nation of us versus them and fuck everybody else. So much so that the normal functioning of our politics, our economy and our society, based on old-fashioned notions of reason, evidence and a fair go for all, start to slide out the door. Imperceptibly at first, then faster and faster as commonly held assumptions about what is right and wrong, and what is true and false, begin to fray. I believe we are now in just such a time. We are beginning to see the radical Americanisation of Australian politics.

My argument is that this need not be the case. Yes, there are many forces at work that are beyond our control which can, and do, make us anxious for our future. These include the big five: pandemics; global financial crises; the great economic, social and job disruptions brought about by artificial intelligence (AI) and technological change; the rise and rise of China; and, of course, the mounting planetary spectre of climate change. There are smaller threats as well, often felt personally, but usually tracing their way back to these mega-trends of our age. Any analysis of Maslow's hierarchy of needs would place each of these close to our most basic human fears about death, dying and disease, about whether we will have a job and an income tomorrow, as well as deeper threats to our underlying sense of purpose, cultural certainty and national identity.

This all seems decidedly grim. But the truth is that the level of personal anxiety and national dystopia that seems rife in our country today is not justified by the actual circumstances in which we find ourselves. When I hear that younger people are now deciding in increasing numbers not to have children because of their fears for the future, I feel that we're racing towards a tipping point of personal and national despair that ignores the great opportunities for reform and renewal that still lie before us. Yes, the challenges are great. But history teaches us that with the right strategy, we are more than capable of navigating each of them. Progress is still possible. The progressive idea is not yet dead. We haven't reached a new, calamitous 'end of history' heralding the death of the enlightenment project. Even a moment's reflection on where we have come from as a human family over just the last hundred years, given the levels of death, disease and poverty that haunted previous generations, should put pay to the pessimism contagion of our current age.

There are those among us, however, whose mission is not to solve these problems but to manipulate them, exacerbating fear, anxiety and uncertainty for a much narrower set of political purposes. These are the professional fearmongers of our age and they know exactly what they are doing. Their mission is simple: to so paralyse the people with fear that it induces a psychological reaction on the part of the voting public that causes them to cling to conservative politics, under the illusion that, by doing so, certainty can somehow magically be restored. Their mission is not to produce policies that deal with the fundamentals of the great change-drivers that are now sweeping over us, or to help navigate our way through them. No, it is simply to use fear to obtain and sustain political power as an end in itself, and to use that power to advantage, often corruptly, the financial interests of the elites that fund them. The purpose of politics for Australia's conservative Coalition is no longer to offer an alternative ideology, strategy or policy for the nation's future, or to help Menzies' 'forgotten people'. The Liberals have now been taken over by a new generation of 'marketing men' (of whom Morrison is the living personification) who believe in nothing other than the campaign science of how to obtain and sustain power at any price, and then run government as an increasingly corrupt syndicate that serves the interests of the most powerful. That is where the political neuroscience of anxiety and fear, its impact on the human brain, and the triumph of emotion over reason come into play. It's the critical alchemy of conservative political success. It's why political strategist Lynton Crosby was knighted by the British Conservatives. And it's why, behind closed doors, the giant cynical joke that leaves the Liberal Party and the Murdoch editors rolling around the floor with laughter, election after election, is this: they can't believe their luck that, just by deploying the politics of anxiety and fear, they manage to get a majority of Australia's working families to look past their own interests and values, and vote instead for a party that is only interested in its own elites.

But none of this would be possible without Liberal Party campaign technology being aided and abetted by the Murdoch media. It is important for both the Labor Party and the millions of Australians who support it to understand that News Corp can no longer be treated seriously as a media company. It is in effect a political party in active pursuit of its own far-right ideology and the active defence of its business interests. For decades, it has acted as the de-facto coalition partner of the US Republicans (helping to deliver the Iraq War; the right-wing takeover of the Republican Party by the Tea Party; and the Trump presidency, whose platform was Murdoch's Fox), the British Conservatives (Boris Johnson and Brexit) and the Australian Liberal Party (successive conservative election victories). The same applies to Murdoch's doctrinaire hostility to any government acting on climate change, thereby skewing the climate debates in both the United States and Australia in a radically denialist direction. For these reasons, it beggars belief that Labor politicians continue to treat Murdoch, his editors and journalists with any level of professional respect. Murdoch's mission is not to hold the Labor Party accountable. It is to destroy the Labor Party as a viable platform for government once and for all. On this the evidence is clear: in the nineteen state and federal elections held over the last ten years, Murdoch's daily papers not only editorialised in support of the Liberal Party. His news organisation campaigned against the Labor Party just as hard as the Liberals did, and in active collaboration with them. No-one disputes these facts anymore. So much so that the Murdoch media have become so arrogant, they have long ceased even trying to pretend they are in any way objective. And given that Lachlan Murdoch has been running the Australian operation on his father's behalf for the better part of a decade, any romantic notion that their media organisation's political mission will soften once Murdoch senior is dead is arrant nonsense. It is simply an excuse for continuing inertia.

For Murdoch, and the two-thirds of the Australian print media he controls, the technique is simple. First, there is unapologetic bias in the news coverage. Second, there is unapologetic bias in editorial opinion, to the point that editorial opinion and news coverage become one. Third, there is the delegitimisation of almost everything the Labor movement stands for— past, present and future—in particular its leadership. John Howard is a protected species. So is Abbott. And now, so is Morrison. Whereas Labor leaders of the last decade are held to be collectively guilty for most of the country's current ills. It's a relentless morality play with a wonderfully predictable script: Labor bad, Liberal good, and the rest is detail. Fourth, the Liberal Party and its leadership is protected from any effective scrutiny of its policies, performance and probity. Indeed, the growing incidence of official corruption at the federal level is occurring in part because the Liberal Party has progressively neutered the independence of the Australian public service and its in-built accountability mechanisms. But the removal of these internal scrutiny mechanisms from within government has been complemented by a Murdoch media that deliberately minimises its coverage of Liberal Party corruption scandals. Furthermore, Murdoch actively collaborates with the government to 'agenda shift' away from these scandals, if and when they are reported by the rest of the media. Finally, once Murdoch prints what he defines as the major story of the day, his editors then seek to set the national political agenda for all that follows in both the electronic and social media. This is not just confined to the conservative echo chamber of right-wing, 2GB radio shock jocks and Sky television. It has a broader effect because Murdoch knows that, across the electronic media in general, independent journalists are now thin on the ground. It's just so easy to 'rip and read' the story of the day, taking your lead from what is already screaming at you across the front pages of the Murdoch print media that morning.

On top of these specific techniques to skew the political debate in favour of the Liberal Party, there is also a subtle, more general strategy that seeks to shape the overall national mood. The unstated objective here is to heighten people's anxieties and fears on a continuing basis, and to do so across a standard range of fabricated concerns: the level of debt (no longer relevant since the Liberals sextupled it); the size of the federal deficit (no longer relevant for the same reason); the threat of heavy-handed, authoritarian government (only applying to state government coronavirus lockdowns, not to the federal government, despite Australia's draconian policy of banning its nationals from leaving the country); fear of the economic and employment impact of any government action on climate change (particularly in regional New South Wales and Queensland, where the only possible economic future is deemed to be coal); and fear of an Asian invasion (first refugees, then Chinese investment, now followed by 'China' in all its forms). Then, of course, there is 'Old Faithful' in the conservative political arsenal: immigration, Islam and terrorism. This is despite the fact that in the twenty years since September 11, owing to the good work of our police and intelligence agencies, there has not been a single mass-casualty attack on Australian soil. Murdoch,

Morrison and Dutton, however, are always there to remind the nation that the threat remains universal, immediate and lethal. This serves their conservative political agenda, irrespective of the operational reality, or whether the agencies may have urged these politicians not to offer ongoing public commentary on the subject. The common denominator in all these domains, however, is a rolling Murdoch editorial and news campaign around national, economic and personal security. It is designed to heighten peoples' awareness of risks and threats, to cause people to be frightened of them, and to remind the electorate that when push comes to shove, only one political party has 'safe hands' in all this. And surprise, surprise, it's not Labor.

The idea, therefore, that the Murdoch media, at least under our current media laws, will ever give the Labor Party a fair go is laughable. Beyond Labor's political interests, however, Murdoch also represents a structural danger to the wider democracy itself. The absence of anything approaching a media level playing field corrupts the entire system. All politics ultimately becomes beholden to the Murdoch syndicate. But rather than be cowed by this, as a number of Labor leaders have been before, or believe that we can do a deal with it, my argument is that we should treat it for what it is. We should be loud and proud and declare open warfare on Murdoch and all that he stands for, through all the media at our collective disposal. In fact, we are wimps if we don't. The Murdoch media have long behaved as bullies. And bullies must be stood up to. There is no downside. The truth is Murdoch seeks to destroy Labor's reputation as a party, as a movement and as a body of progressive ideas. We are perfectly entitled, based on the facts alone, to go on the attack. Whether we like it or not, we are in a war against Murdoch. And the sooner we realise this the better. After all, these are the terms of engagement Murdoch himself set against Labor more than a decade ago. And increasingly, we also underestimate how uncomfortably the level of stench that now rises from the Murdoch media already sits with much of the Australian public. The Australian people have never forgotten the man who, thirty years ago, traded in his Australian identity to become an American media billionaire.

So what of the rest of the Australian media landscape? The picture there is also decidedly bleak.

Over the last several years, Murdoch, supported by a series of decisions by the Australian Competition and Consumer Commission (ACCC), has expanded his national reach and penetration. The most significant ACCC decision came in 2016, when Murdoch was allowed to buy Australian Provincial Newspapers (APN), thereby adding another 102 titles to his stable across regional Australia. The anti-competitive impact of this decision in Queensland was acute, surrendering dozens of proudly independent mastheads to Murdoch's ultimate editorial control. There was zero business case for this purchase, given that the rates of financial return for these papers was low against investment alternatives for News Corp. But the political rate of return was high given that Murdoch was now able to campaign for the Liberal and National parties across the most decentralised state in the Commonwealth, where so many federally significant swing-seats lie outside the capital city. At the time of the APN purchase, Murdoch promised the moon, including major new investments in regional papers with 'strategies to generate further growth'. The reality, however, has been the reverse. Under cover of COVID-19, Murdoch in June 2020 closed down eleven of these papers altogether, and ended print coverage in twenty-two cases, migrating the entire product online. This was among 126 papers nationally that were either closed or moved totally online. Editorial control was vested to a central newsroom in Brisbane, thereby enabling an approved central message to be disseminated across the state whenever needed.

Murdoch's consolidation of media power in Australia hasn't stopped with APN. His March 2020 decision to abandon News Corp's investment in Australian Associated Press (AAP) and set up his own rival wire service was an attempt to destroy one of the few remaining independent news voices in the country. Once again, this was done under cover of the COVID-19 crisis. AAP, which was established in 1935, has been particularly important for regional papers, which are unable to support their own nation-wide network of reporters. The Murdoch intention is to replicate the AAP model 'in house' and sell approved News Corp product to news outlets across the entire country. As AAP struggles to remain afloat after Murdoch's disinvestment, the immediate impact of this decision on media diversity is already acute.

The number of voices heard across the Australian media landscape has continued to contract.

But what of Fairfax and its major mastheads *The Sydney Morning Herald*, Melbourne's *Age*, the *Financial Review* and online publications such as the *Brisbane Times*? These were credibly independent news and editorial platforms until the ACCC's decision in 2018 to allow Nine Entertainment to buy them out. Since then, all four publications have slowly drifted further to the right under the stewardship of Nine Entertainment's 'independent' chair Peter Costello, a former Liberal Party deputy leader. The *Financial Review* has always been a hard-right paper in its news and editorial coverage, although it does permit different views to be published on its editorial pages. If there was any doubt on this question, Nine's decision to host a major fundraiser at its Sydney premises for Morrison and the rest of the Liberal Party leadership straight after the 2019 federal election, provided definitive evidence of this entrenched political bias. No such invitation had ever been extended to the Labor Party by either Nine or the previous owners of Fairfax. As for *The Guardian*, although its marketplace is the political centre and centre-left, it has never had a print newspaper in Australia and its online penetration is currently ranked only fourth across the country.

So in terms of what's left of the Australian media terrain, it's principally Channel Seven, Channel Ten, the ABC and SBS that offer the potential for anything approaching fair and balanced coverage for the progressive centre of Australian politics. Once again, however, the operational reality is troubling. Take Channel Seven, whose owner and chairman Kerry Stokes made plain his own personal views against the Labor Party during his famous leaked conversation with Rupert Murdoch in the lead-up to the 2019 federal election. Channel Ten, which has the lowest ratings of all five Australian networks, is routinely in and out of receivership and invests very little in its news and current affairs services.

That brings us to the ABC, which both the Liberal Party and the Murdoch Party have long seen as their ideological and commercial nemesis. The Liberals have deployed every power at their disposal to bring the ABC to heal under their newly appointed Chair Ita Buttrose and the Director of News, Analysis and Investigations Gaven Morris. The Morrison government has ignored the laws introduced by my government to ensure that the ABC board was depoliticised, by having recommendations for appointments put forward to the communications minister by an independent panel. They have slashed total funding to the ABC by $783 million, or more than 10 per cent of its operational budget. In implementing these cuts, ABC management has focused their efforts on news and current affairs programming, thereby reducing further the level of independent journalistic scrutiny of government policy and performance. Murdoch, in the meantime, has waged a long-term campaign against the very existence of public broadcasters, both in Australia and the United Kingdom, and has applied continuing political pressure to the Liberal government to bring the ABC to heal. Yet, despite multiple public attacks on the broadcaster by the Murdoch media, the ABC has rarely, if ever, used its current affairs or investigative units to probe the extraordinary political influence that News Corp wields over Australian politics and governments. Murdoch himself, despite his singular power, has been a virtual no-go zone for ABC investigative or general reporting, for fear of retribution. The overall effect of these factors on the national broadcaster has been threefold: an ever-reducing budget, the reallocation of these reduced resources away from news and current affairs, and the steady shifting of the ABC's editorial and news coverage towards the political right. As for Sky News Australia, now wholly owned by Murdoch, it has simply become the broadcast arm of News Corp's national propaganda broadsheet *The Australian*.

Radio in Australia is dominated by the ABC and the decisively right-wing, Nine-owned Macquarie national radio network. ABC radio news and current affairs is shaped by the same forces at work within ABC television. Meanwhile, Macquarie has become home to shock-jock broadcasters in Sydney at 2GB, Melbourne at 3AW and Brisbane at 4BC, where the interconnections with the Murdoch print media on key personnel appointments, news content and editorial bias are crystal clear. The net effect is that whatever is printed in the Murdoch media, particularly in the three state capitals that matter most in terms of the numbers of seats in the Australian parliament, is then rebroadcast across the 2GB network nationwide, capturing both morning and afternoon drive-time audiences, and thereby reinforcing the overall content of News Corp's pro-Liberal, anti-Labor message.

The final piece in the Australian media puzzle is the social media platforms owned by the emerging monopoly corporations Google and Facebook. Social media has contributed to a plethora of new media voices across Australian politics. It has challenged the traditional Murdoch monopoly by empowering individuals to work around the choke points of control that News Corp's printing presses and editorial control have represented in the past. But it has also created a new, unprecedented power for the major digital platforms and their ability to deploy algorithm-driven content targeted to specified political and commercial audiences, and available to the highest bidder. This, therefore, provides hyper-platforms for the best-funded of the political parties on the Australian landscape—usually the Liberal Party. Google and Facebook represent a whole new generation of challenges to the power of the media in any modern democracy. First, it brings into new and urgent focus the factual accuracy of reporting, opinion and advertising (and the increasing convergence of all three), magnifying longstanding tensions between freedom of expression, fact-checking by editorial departments and outright defamation. In addition, the Google and

Facebook platforms, because of their open-access regimes, have already shown themselves to be open to large-scale foreign or corporate manipulation. Finally, traditional media companies, led by Murdoch's News Corp, have attacked Google and Facebook for 'stealing' their content by distributing it online. Murdoch has demanded that the digital giants pay News Corp for any content that appears on their platforms, and that they also provide deeper information about the algorithms they use for the distribution of their product. The Morrison government, ever-attentive to Murdoch's demands, has now released the legislative draft of a new 'News Media Bargaining Code' which would provide News Corp with everything it has sought from the digital majors. The Labor Party is not a friend of any monopoly, traditional or digital. But to further empower the Murdoch media by having the government intervene on Murdoch's behalf to force the digital giants to give News Corp a new revenue stream, and to grant them access to information about algorithms that would enhance their ability to target the Australian public, is not in the national interest. Murdoch's ability to use and abuse his existing monopoly powers would be turbocharged.

For these reasons, while Murdoch's power in Australian politics is *already* a threat to our democracy because his editors refuse to provide a level playing field, this power is set to become even greater. It is anchored in his print monopoly. It extends into television. News Corp has a strategic alliance across radio through the 2GB network, which faithfully reproduces its content. It is seeking to become a major digital media player in its own right, in large part by using its relationship with the Morrison government to undermine the business models of both Google and Facebook. Murdoch has also successfully lobbied the federal government to weaken the ABC's independence by cutting its funding and influencing its editorial position in a direction conducive to the overall conservative cause. To add insult to injury, Morrison has also gifted $40 million to Murdoch's Foxtel, allegedly to broadcast women's sport. Moreover, Murdoch has created a political–media dynasty set to last another forty years under Lachlan, and presumably his own heirs and successors. And the idea that the Australian Press Council will protect the Australian public and the wider Australian democracy against Murdoch's abuse of his monopoly powers is simply risible.

The cancer Murdoch represents at the heart of our political system is set to metastasise. Unless we act.

Acting against Murdoch takes courage. Real courage. That's because his stock-in-trade is to inflict damage on those who dare to attack him, or those who seek to reduce his power in the international media market. There has already been clear evidence of that in the United Kingdom with the 2011 Leveson Inquiry into Murdoch's phone-hacking scandal. Murdoch also attacked the 2012 Finkelstein Inquiry in Australia into the concentration of media power. Part of Murdoch's modus operandi is to create a climate of fear. As one News Corp journalist said recently in a BBC documentary on Murdoch's abuse of media power in that country, having Murdoch on your trail is like having an entire division of Hitler's SS seeking to destroy you. The same applies in Australia. This is a major problem for the political class, where generations of Labor politicians have been taught not to rock the boat against Murdoch's interests through any legislative or regulatory change. Murdoch's approach has also been to offer a form of 'protection' to certain select Labor politicians by giving them positive coverage (or at least an implicit guarantee of limited negative coverage) if they keep

Murdoch's editors informed of confidential debates within the party's leadership circle, particularly as they relate to any efforts that impact Murdoch's commercial interests. This has included television rights for the coverage of major sporting events through Murdoch's once-profitable Foxtel cable network. It also includes any proposals to change the current laws and regulations that govern Australia's media industry, impacting Murdoch's monopoly position.

The fear factor that Murdoch generates is not limited to Australian politics. The same applies to any business competitor, academic inquiry (how often do you see major university research projects that seriously examine Murdoch's media monopoly?) or the rest of journalism. Journalists actively fear being targeted by Murdoch. In a limited media market, Murdoch is capable of destroying journalists' career prospects if they take on the Royal Family of Australian media politics. It is a telling example that the ABC's *Four Corners*, the national broadcaster's premier investigative program, has never produced a report on Murdoch's abuse of media power in Australia. Murdoch has effectively become untouchable for Australian politics, the academy and journalism because people fear the consequences for their reputations and their careers if they cross him. Increasingly, it feels like being controlled by a local variant of the Sicilian mafia. For these reasons, we need to be clear about three things. First, the Murdoch media will not change. Second, the Murdoch media monopoly represents a growing but largely unreported threat to the future lifeblood of our democracy, as he loads the media dice each day in favour of the hard right of Australian politics, while his editors turn a blind eye to Liberal Party incompetence and institutional corruption as part of an unspoken deal with the conservatives. Third, for the Labor Party in particular, Murdoch now represents an existential threat to its ability to ever be returned to national government. This is because of his proven capacity to run vicious, continuous campaigns against us, both federally and at the state level, and where possible to divide us internally. One objective of this continuing abuse of Murdoch's media power, for example, is for Australia to never take effective action on climate change, given that climate change denialism is a fundamental credo for both Murdoch senior and junior.

Labor can ignore all this and accept the reality that it is likely to sentence us to permanent opposition.

Or we can summon the courage to take action. I recommend a four-part approach to taking action:

- the organisation of a mass nationwide campaign against Murdoch, with the objective of establishing a Commonwealth royal commission (or, in its absence, a state one) to investigate fully and openly Murdoch's abuse of his monopoly media power for political and commercial gain, and his abuse of press standards as enshrined in journalists' professional code of ethics, and to make recommendations for Australian media law that will guarantee maximum media ownership diversity for the future
- the mobilisation of national and global shareholder action in relation to News Corp, given that organisation's doctrinal opposition to climate change action
- the encouragement of Australian industry funds to invest in a major alternative media platform in order to maximise Australia's national media diversity
- the legislative entrenchment of a long-term funding formula for the ABC.

None of these approaches is of itself a silver bullet to the heart of the Murdoch beast. But all are necessary to change the media balance of power. Neither the ACCC nor our existing media owner-ship laws have done the job of ensuring reasonable media diversity to safeguard the long-term interests of the Australian democracy. An appropriately qual-ified royal commissioner will be able to examine media ownership and diversity models in other democracies around the world, as well as the future of public interest journalism. The commissioner will also be able to examine the media's enforcement of its own professional standards, including require-ments for separating editorial and news reporting, and honest reporting and fact-checking across all platforms—print, broadcasting, radio, digital and social. The future of public broadcasting will need to be addressed, including entrenching ABC budget growth in legislation, creating an effective Senate veto over funding cuts. Existing legislation for the editorial independence of the ABC will also need to be strengthened to prevent the type of politicisation of the public broadcaster that has occurred under the current Liberal government. As for global shareholder action, close scrutiny should be paid to the News Corp share register to bring pressure to bear on the most egregious behaviours of the Murdoch family in their long-running campaign against effective climate change action around the world. Finally, the time has come for the Australian industry funds, given their trillions of dollars of invested capital and their trade union origins, to consider other measures to protect the broader interests of their members. The Murdoch media, in partnership with the Liberal government, have conducted a systematic campaign over a decade to reduce working families' superannuation. The industry funds should therefore consider their own investment in a national news media organisation to help restore balance to the Australian political debate. This would require the consent of the majority of policyholders. It might also require legislative change to enable funds to make investments in social enterprises for, say, up to 1 per cent of their entire portfolio—if such investments are deemed by trustees to be critical to the interests of policyholders.

There is a simple truth at stake in all this. Murdoch and Morrison both understand the absolute central-ity of the power of the media to Australian politics.

At present, they control it. Unless the Labor Party, the labour movement and progressive politics in general understand this fundamental truth and act on it, there will never be another long-term, sustainable federal Labor government in Australia. The temptation of the Labor Party is always to direct its energies to new leadership, new policy or even new campaign technology. These may be useful. But they do not deal with the underlying political reality that ultimately determines whether any of these changes will be electorally effective. And that is that the media dice are loaded against us, and this provides a massive, built-in advantage for the conservatives that has become increasingly difficult to breach. To take on Murdoch in a full-blooded assault will take courage. But there is now no alternative. Not just for progressive politics, but for the future of the democratic project itself. Otherwise, we permanently surrender power to an unelected syndicate.

AND JUST WHAT DOES THE LIBERAL PARTY NOW STAND FOR?

Politics, properly defined, should be both a positive and a negative equation: to argue for our proposition for how to shape Australia's future in national security, the economy, individual enterprise, social justice and the environment, as well as to demolish the conservatives' proposition for the same. Over the last decade or more, the Labor Party has dedicated the bulk of its political energies to the former, but with insufficient attention to the latter. By contrast, the Liberal Party has had no such qualms. The Liberals since Hewson have never had a proactive policy vision for Australia's future. Their single interest has been to destroy whatever policies the previous Labor government has put in place, and to run a continuing negative campaign against everything the Labor Party stands for, with the single objective of obtaining and sustaining political power. Any passing examination of Abbott's election program for the 2013 federal election, and the subsequent actions taken during his term, demonstrate this central point. The same occurred in both the 2016 and 2019 elections. The facts, as evidenced by the content of election advertisements and the Liberals' election manifesto, demonstrate that the Liberal Party is an overwhelmingly negative political operation. In this, their reliable Coalition partner has been the Murdoch media and its relentless negative campaigns against Labor leadership and policy. And the bottom line is that this combined, relentless, negative assault has been highly politically effective. The essential learning for the Labor Party is that, as a movement, we must radically lift our negative game. We will never secure an election victory in order to deliver our program based simply on the goodness of our hearts, the righteousness of our cause or the intellectual rigour of our policies. This readjustment of the Labor Party's political strategy, to fully embrace negative campaigning, will take courage too, because it requires a departure from the comfortable, comforting but self-defeating ways of the past. It requires that we become as brutal in our politics as the Liberals and Murdoch have been towards us for decades. Although in our case, we can do so without resorting to the outright lying of our opponents. The truth, effectively told, is already powerful enough for our purposes.

This focused, negative campaign against our opponents should be deployed at three levels: the collapse of the entire conservative ideological project in the aftermath of the COVID-19 crisis; the real nature of Liberal values as those of a party that consistently preferences the powerful over those just trying to stay afloat; and a potent cocktail of Liberal Party hypocrisy, waste and corruption. Each of these elements is important in its own right because each deals with different aspects of the political marketplace. Together, however, they form a powerful political narrative. This is not just aimed at winning the intellectual argument. It is also aimed at winning the battle of raw emotions. That's because it is both these faculties—reason and emotion—that ultimately determine people's voting behaviour. If politics was simply a debating society, where reasonable argument determined the day, Labor would have prevailed in virtually every election. But it's not.

As noted earlier in this account, the Liberals, to compensate for their yawning deficit in ideas, vision and policy, and to camouflage the regressive nature of their substantive program in government, have mastered the alchemy of anxiety, fear, anger and even rage. Their purpose is to focus people's attention elsewhere and to galvanise voting behaviour accordingly. The longstanding response from progressive politicians has been to counter the politics of fear with the politics of hope. But the ugly reality is that anxiety and fear are far more potent emotions than hope, a task made easier by the underlying uncertainties of our age and the flight to certainty and security, however illusory, that these induce. Therefore, the Labor project must embrace with equal passion and execution *both* a positive agenda of hope *as well as* a negative agenda. This should target the conservative's naked greed, self-interest, indifference to working people's lives, and contempt for those who need support to survive, as well as their rank hypocrisy in pretending to defend the interests of what was once described as the 'Howard battlers'. Our political mission is to counter the conservatives' emotional assault, driven by anxiety, with our own ability to mobilise people's anger at what the conservatives are actually doing to diminish their wages, salaries, working conditions and retirement income—while increasing the cost of their education, health, child care and aged care. It is also to explain that, while attacking the living standards of working families, these very same conservatives are delivering tax cuts to those who do not need them, and providing financial benefits, often corruptly, to their inner political circle. In other words, our job is to prise open people's anger by simply telling the truth about what is being done to them by a Liberal Party which ultimately has no interest at all in your average hardworking Australian. And then—and only then— our responsibility is to offer these very same people real hope for the future with a positive policy program that delivers both support for them *and* strength for the nation.

The Liberals' overall ideological project is now, almost literally, bankrupt. The Liberals have campaigned for decades against the Labor Party on the grounds that fiscal stimulus, budget deficits, public debt, public infrastructure investment and industry policy undermine Australia's economic strength by saddling future generations with unsustainable debt. On this basis, the Liberal Party argued for paying off public debt, a return to budget surpluses, deregulation, small government and low taxes as the basis of their claim to be Australia's natural economic managers. We now know this claim to have been a lie from the beginning. The Liberals now report five times the net debt than existed under the last Labor government and seven times the budget deficit, and they have now resumed the core elements of Labor's national infrastructure plan with the proposed completion of the NBN. As a result, the entire edifice of Liberal Party ideology has collapsed, together with the believability of the fear campaigns based on these claims that they have long mounted against the Labor Party. If their critique against the previous Labor government was that we believed in 'big government', by contrast the Liberals now believe in 'giant government'. At the height of the GFC, government expenditure as a proportion of the overall size of the economy peaked at 26 per cent of GDP, whereas in 2020 under the Liberals it reached 35 per cent of GDP. At the height of the GFC, our budget deficit reached 4 per cent of GDP, but in 2020 it exploded to 11 per cent of GDP and rising. By the end of our period in government, our federal net debt stood at 12 per cent of GDP— among the lowest in the Organisation for Economic Co-operation and Development (OECD) and still capable of sustaining the retention of our AAA credit rating—whereas in 2020 our debt-to-GDP ratio climbed to an eye-watering 36 per cent and was expected to rise to above 45 per cent.

By any measure, the entire basis of the Liberal Party's rolling campaigns against Labor's fiscal stimulus, debt and deficit, deliberately aimed at fostering people's anxiety, fear and anger over 'Labor's economic mismanagement', has now been proven to have been a lie all along. Our political task is to force the Liberal Party to admit publicly that this was nothing more than deception, and to ram this home to the voting public, thereby delegitimising any future economic fear campaigns against Labor. Beyond that, our task is also to demonstrate that these facts now establish that Labor in fact has been the party of strong, thoughtful and effective economic management. Labor deployed stimulus, debt and deficit early, effectively and at relatively modest levels. We kept the economy out of recession—unlike the Liberals, who acted late and panicked as the economy tanked before sliding into deeply negative growth, thus placing the nation's global credit rating under greater threat. The time has now come to smash the Liberal Party's ideological and economic credentials, and to use this period to turn the tables once and for all.

Furthermore, the collapse of the Liberal Party's political masking device on debt, deficit and the economy does not mean that the Liberals have abandoned the remainder of their ideological crusade against the interests of working families. Remember, the whole purpose of their decade-long campaign to cause the voting public to fear Labor on economic management was to camouflage the Liberals' real political agenda. This agenda has had three parts: to boost the profit share for big business by reducing the wages share, working conditions and superannuation; to deliver tax cuts to those who don't need them, and to pay for these by undermining income support for struggling families, child care, the aged pension, health, education, disability and aged care; and to prevent action on climate change in order to protect the Liberals' financial supporters through yet another fear campaign, arguing falsely that taking action to reduce greenhouse gases (GHGs) and increase renewables would damage the economy and employment. All three of these Liberal agendas, when stripped to their essentials, are driven by individual greed. This, in reality, is the core Liberal value. But because it is such an ugly value which cannot be owned overtly, Liberal strategy has always been to mask it by any other distracting device possible. As noted above, this has included a wide range of campaigns all aimed at stoking a cocktail of anxiety, fear, anger, rage and xenophobia on the part of the voting public. They do this by directing people's attention to 'welfare entitlement and fraud',

'Asian investors taking our prime agricultural land', 'refugees and immigrants taking our jobs', 'foreign threats to our fundamental national security', as well as 'a politically correct', now 'woke', culture that undermines our Australian sense of cultural identity. None of these claims can be substantiated with any credible, measurable evidence. They are political inventions. Nonetheless, because the Liberals are now denied their traditional reliance on debt, deficit and the economy, these other fear-based campaigns are likely to be intensified further. For the Liberals, on these issues, as with the economy, the truth does not matter. What matters is the psychological admixture of a rolling campaign that prevents people from focusing on the erosion of their real living standards, the content of their safety net, and whether or not there will be a sustainable climate for their kids' future. Labor's urgent task is to relentlessly drill home this great Liberal deception. It is also to focus on the deep values divide which lies beneath this debate—one that the Liberals will do anything to hide. The Liberals' essential values remain individual and corporate greed. These stand in fundamental opposition to the much deeper and widely held Australian value of a fair go for all. This means a fair go for the millions of Australians who are wage and salary earners, small business owners and individual contractors, as well as a fair go for the next generation of Australians by safeguarding a climate that can sustain them for the century that lies ahead.

There is a further, sinister dimension of the Liberal Party in power that now needs to be brought to the surface of the Australian political debate. And that is corruption. The absence of Murdoch media scrutiny, a cowed ABC and an increasingly politicised public service have created structural factors that have increased the incidence of official corruption at the federal level. This has not been the case in the past, when our national institutions have historically functioned well, thereby preserving Australia's hard-won reputation as one of the cleanest countries in the world. However, the most recent reporting by Transparency International has seen Australia steadily falling down the 'clean government' scale as a culture of corruption has begun to take root. Former conservative ministers have flouted official guidelines to become lobbyists or contractors to corporations which directly benefit from Australian Government decisions. Government contracts have been executed without proper tendering processes, often to the direct financial benefit of Liberal Party donors. The auditor-general's office is being denied the funds to do its job properly, with many regular audits left undone. The links between the Liberal Party in power and the Murdoch media's commercial interests have also been seen. Direct government payments have been made to Fox without tender. The Liberal government also undermined the last Labor government's $43 billion fibre-to-the-premises NBN with a copper substitute, thereby extending the life of Murdoch's Fox cable monopoly by discouraging streaming services from fully entering the Australian market. These factors have all been compounded by the Liberals' refusal to support substantive campaign finance reform. There has been a growing stench in Australian federal politics over the last seven years. Labor's task is not just to respond to the problem by offering an earnest public policy undertaking to establish a meaningful federal anti-corruption commission if and when we next form government, although this is now necessary. Labor's immediate political task is to heighten the Australian people's growing sense of disgust at what is now happening behind closed doors in Australian conservative politics. Greed is not just a Liberal value. It is also generating corrupt behaviour at the national level of an order of magnitude never before seen in our country. This is part of the moral armoury we will need to drive the Liberal Party from office.

Labor's responsibility, therefore, is to weave these various elements together into a compelling, negative narrative on why the Liberals are no longer fit for office. And not just at the exhaustion of their 'natural' political cycle every decade or so, when the electorate finally decides that 'it's time', albeit briefly, before the next cycle of conservative government begins after a term or two of Labor. No, our responsibility is to demonstrate their unfitness for office for the long term. Within a Labor Party subculture that constantly gravitates towards the intellectualisation of everything, one predisposed to even more fevered work to develop policy perfection from opposition, to embark on a sustained, negative campaign to demolish the Liberal Party will take energy, discipline and, again, courage. The secret, unstated hope of many within the Labor subculture is that 'anybody else other than me' should do the negative campaigning, for fear that it taints their own long-term career prospects. That's because the commentariat find negative campaigning distasteful. The dinner-party circuit also finds it distasteful. While they may agree with your private critique of the government, they will run a million miles from any public attack. We are also constantly being told that the voting public dislike 'being negative'. But if negative campaigning is so bad, then why do the conservatives spend so much time on it? It's because they know it works. And it is one of the reasons they have been in power for two-thirds of the history of the federation, and ourselves for only one-third. For Labor, therefore, to abandon the task to others because it is seen to be personally or politically distasteful is little more than a dereliction of duty. Every member of the front bench and every member of the parliamentary party must have the evisceration of the Liberal Party as a primary responsibility. This does not mean we need to lie as the conservatives do. What it does mean is to tell the unvarnished truth about the fraudulence of Liberal Party ideology, the self-centred greed that lies at the heart of Liberal 'values', as well as the Liberal government's growing corruption of the essential institutions of our Commonwealth. And the only way to prevail in this debate is to deploy every rational *and* emotional lever at our disposal. Only then will Labor be able to implement its program for government.

CRAFTING A POLICY VISION FOR AUSTRALIA'S FUTURE: TACKLING THE MEGA-CHALLENGES THAT CONFRONT US

Politics is not the sound of just one hand clapping, whether that hand happens to be negative or positive. It is the sound of two hands clapping—*both* negative *and* positive. Otherwise, for the Labor Party, we lose. To the disappointment of some, however, for Labor our entry point must be negative: to cause the Australian people to question, doubt and reject both the values *and* the policy effectiveness of the entire Liberal Party enterprise. This is necessary so that the people then begin to hear our message on how we will govern differently. Once this window to peoples' hearts and minds is opened, it is important that we have ready our own policy vision for government. This should not be expressed in the usual saccharine language and political banalities of so many of the vision statements of the past. It should be expressed clearly in terms of our values, and how these values are reflected in our policy responses to the great challenges of our time. Too many vision statements avoid the big ones. We should not.

A clear articulation of Labor values is important, differentiating us clearly from the Liberals from the get-go. This should include values of security, prosperity, equality of opportunity, fairness and sustainability. We cannot cede security and prosperity to the Liberals as 'in-built' conservative values, as some on the centre-left are tempted to do. All citizens have a legitimate expectation of being secure, just as they should aspire to individual and national prosperity through their own hard work, enterprise and success. Values of equality, a fair go for all and environmental sustainability are more familiar elements of the Labor repertoire. But if we fail to offer all five values as our foundational message to the Australian people, we will fail. We will be seen as reluctant to embrace the fundamentals of national security and a strong economy as a natural part of our program for government. Besides, our long and distinguished record of government during previous economic and national security crises means we have everything to be proud of on this score, and nothing to be ashamed of.

The world has now entered a twenty-first-century reality that is infinitely less predictable than the world of the second half of the twentieth century. The classic conservative approach to public policy is one that reacts to events as they arise, repudiating any notion of national planning as the stuff of dreamers. Such an approach no longer suits our national needs and purposes, if ever it did. In a quieter, more predictable age, it may have been possible. But this is no longer the case. Australia now confronts a series of global mega-changes that present us with existential challenges to navigate if we are to secure our future. The big five challenges are:

- the need to radically reinvent our long-term growth model, given the impact of the global technology revolution on Australia's future economic competitiveness
- the impact of climate change on sustainable economic development
- the ability of working families to stay afloat amid deep economic crises and declining social equity
- the rise of China
- the management of future global pandemics.

Each of these challenges requires a more antici-patory, better-planned, more reformist agenda than in the past. Our vision for government does not mean that we literally have to 'cover the field' across every portfolio in public administration. In fact, from opposition, it is unwise to do so. People become overwhelmed by too much information. But they do want to know what we will do about the big things that worry them, the things that are the real sources of anxiety rather than the confected ones. That's where the public has a legitimate expectation to understand the broad policy contours of our plan. The alternative for Australia is for the nation simply to consign itself to being tossed about on the wild winds and currents of international change, uncertain of our course, and potentially to our national peril. That is what the Liberal Party has done for decades, relying on such tropes as 'sound judgement' as crises arise, without putting in the hard yards to think these through in advance, or to care about the long-term consequences of their actions. As the alternative government of Australia, the Australian Labor Party will need to craft a policy vision for the future which tackles each of these big challenges.

The Future Drivers of Australian Economic Growth

On growing the economy, the essential challenge for the future is not tax. That is the consistent conservative script. According to the US Congressional Budget Office, Australia has one of the lowest levels of effective business taxation in the OECD. If there are fresh tax measures to consider, they should be to reduce the effective tax impost on small business so that they have the incentive over time to grow into the medium and big businesses of the future. The tax rate for small business should slowly taper up to the normal corporate rate once these businesses have become confident of their future in the marketplace. The uncomfortable truth, as revealed by the 2018 Royal Commission into Misconduct in the Banking, Superannuation and Financial Services Industry, is that the Australian banking industry has, by and large, forced a predatory culture on small business finance. That must change. The Australian finance industry more broadly must realise that its purpose is to serve the needs of the real economy, not just serve itself, by overcharging for the services its says it delivers, while under-financing the sustainable aspirations of the small business sector. The finance industry is licensed by governments to provide these services, not just to provide itself with record levels of remuneration which bear little relationship to the growth of customers' businesses. This too must change. A seminal challenge for the Labor Party is to become the clarion-clear voice of Australian small business through reducing the regulatory burden of the sector while also minimising the tax impost on it. Small businesses are the 'little guys' of the Australian economy who provide the bulk of the nation's employment. They are a natural constituency for the Australian Labor Party. We should champion their success.

Australian big business has always been more than willing in their criticism of governments, in particular Labor governments and the unions. Indeed, their peak bodies have been critical of most other institutions and influences at work in leading the Australian economy—other than themselves. That, of course, is their right. But it's time big business also had it served back to them on their own international competitiveness. Against international benchmarking surveys on management, innovation, entrepreneurialism, export orientation and R&D, much of Australia's corporate leadership does not measure up to most of their international competitors. This stands in stark contrast to the self-congratulatory culture among many corporate leaders, despite suboptimal long-term growth strategies and a general failure to grow market share through exports. It also contrasts with generous remuneration structures which are insufficiently linked to long-term corporate growth, let alone their growth in global markets, but are instead based on short-term share market capitalisation. If you were to survey the Business Council of Australia, for example, on the proportion of Australia's top 100 firms which have chief executives or board members who have served in management positions in Asia—the largest centre of global growth for the twenty-first century— the answer would be thin. Australian corporate elites have remained, in large part, a self-satisfied, white, male enclave for whom Asian markets have proven to be just too hard. Our national corporate culture is, frankly, suburban. We are the only Western country located in Asia, which should provide us with a major natural advantage. But the uncomfortable truth is that, beyond commodities, education and tourism, our corporate performance in the world's largest emerging markets in China, Japan, India and next door in Indonesia has been statistically abysmal. Beyond Asia, the fact that Australia's major corporates have failed to generate a single, universally recognisable global brand since World War II says everything.

One further impediment to economic growth is the rolling failure of Australia's venture capital markets to back local innovation. The loss of Australian intellectual property (IP) abroad is the continuing tragedy of much of our postwar economic history. Wi-fi is the most recent case in point. Developed in large part in Australia, this critical innovation was lost abroad in 1999 because of a failure to locate sufficient venture capital to take it to the global market. Imagine the branding opportunities for Australia if this had become one of ours around the world. Everybody uses wi-fi. It could have become our very own Apple. The loss of such opportunities in information technology, biotechnology, nanotechnology, new materials research, AI, blockchain technology and big data must stop. We have five of the world's top 100 research universities. We also host world-class biomedical research institutes in our major cities, which produce world-class research and innovation. Yet the constant failure lies on the entrepreneurial and venture capital side in not allowing this innovation to realise its full market potential using Australian firms—and returning the profits to Australia. Governments cannot mandate the banks, or our broader corporate leadership, to adopt a more creative approach to national wealth generation. But because the nation's superannuation funds, both public and private, benefit from a legislated superannuation guarantee levy, the time has come to consider mandating a small percentage of their combined investments to be directed to local venture capital projects in order to commercialise Australian-sourced innovation. Although representing a tiny amount for each fund, given the overall size of the industry, in aggregate this would create sufficient critical mass in the venture capital industry in this country to meet the demand of our innovators, who are hungry for new investment. This could make a strategic difference if funds are forced to work hard to find new investments from our thousands of innovators in generating new sources of long-term wealth for their members. The funds, of course, will scream about the impact any such directive would have on their fiduciary duty to maximise returns to policyholders. They scream less, however, when these returns are compromised by the fees structure these same fund managers happily impose on a generally unwitting public.

On the impact of technological change on existing industries and employment, the challenge of course is large. Given that these changes are likely to gather in pace rather than the reverse, there are five types of responses necessary for Australia. The first is a large scale reinvestment in STEM subjects (science, technology, engineering and mathematics) across the school, further education and higher education systems. All other serious countries are doing this. Australia, according to rankings released by the OECD's Programme for International Student Assessment, is now falling behind. This must be urgently reversed as a strategic national priority. Second, the creation of a critical mass in Australian venture capital funds, as recommended above, is urgent. This is the only way new jobs will be created in new technology industries. Third, the centrality of AI, big data and blockchain to the next industrial revolution means that the world will be divided between those whose economies can generate and manipulate data across all industry applications, and those who do not own any of these processes—or the IP that supports them. This will be the future determinant of national wealth and power and the competitiveness of nations. Australia is rapidly being left behind. Government, in partnership with our best research institutes and private firms, must now take the lead, given that our private sector has not yet risen to the challenge. Fourth, given the growing likelihood of major employment disruptions though automation, IT and AI, Australia will need a new National Jobs and Training Agency to provide retrenched or otherwise longer-term unemployed workers with a universal training guarantee for newly emerging industries, as well as to place retrained workers in new jobs within a specified period of time. At present, the training and employment functions of government agencies are separate, underfunded and ineffectively incentivised. They must be brought together with a new, demanding mandate, and with the resources necessary to give effect to that mandate. Failure to do this effectively will result in a growing generation of unemployed and alienated Australians who no longer have a stake in the country's future.

Finally, and perhaps most controversially, I believe we must aim to build a Big Australia. Neither maximum workforce participation nor productivity growth alone will generate an economy large enough and a workforce young enough to pay for the country's future. The ageing of our population is real. The impact on future retirement income, health and aged-care costs will be prohibitive. These cannot be wished away. This leaves to one side funding the future cost of our national defence in an increasingly uncertain and unstable region and world. For Australia to sustain its future standard of living and meet its future social policy and national security policy needs, we will need a much larger population. That's why we need to plan effectively for an optimum population size. A Big Australia is not incompatible with properly mandated urban planning, infrastructure development and environmental sustainability. Nor is it incompatible with the development of new population centres in the water-rich northern parts of the country. Nor does it prevent mandating new migrants to move to these regions rather than the capital cities to avoid overcrowding. All this is doable—and at a pace and composition of migration flows that maintains social stability on the way through. Of course, there will be vigorous reaction to this proposal. There has been in the past, most of it ill-informed populism. That's because everybody is running for cover while no-one is answering the core question: in the absence of continuing significant migration flows, who on earth is going to pay for our most fundamental future national needs, from health and aged care to retirement incomes to national defence? We run the risk of being a young country which becomes old before its time. These are the seeds of national decline.

To accompany this, we will need an even more robust Infrastructure Australia to ensure we have the roads, railways, ports, electricity supply, water supply, waste-management systems and high-speed broadband to meet the future needs of a growing nation. The conservatives have effectively destroyed the NBN as an effective fibre-to-the-premises network nationwide. We will have to rebuild it or we will fall even further behind as the rest of the world pivots massively to digital. Infrastructure Australia will also need new sources of infrastructure financing. New types of nation-building bonds will be needed, with returns comparable to those offered for regular

Australian Government paper. This will be necessary if the big projects of the future (for example, high-speed rail between our major capital cities) are ever to be built. Otherwise, we will be full of plans but with limited finance to give them effect. And our growth potential will be strangled as a result.

Climate Change, Sustainable Growth and Australian Global Climate Leadership

Australia must transform itself by mid-century into a net-zero-emissions economy. With the right policy settings, this is entirely compatible with building a much bigger Australia. We need a globally competitive carbon price set through the market mechanism of an emissions trading scheme. We will also need to maintain and expand the existing Renewable Energy Target. Solar panels should become a mandatory part of the national building code for all new structures—residential and non-residential. Incentives should be provided from the retrofitting of the existing national housing stock that has not had solar energy installed under previous Labor government programs. And the government should directly fund the installation of solar energy equipment in public housing, ensuring that the most vulnerable, who struggle with our country's high energy prices, immediately see a reduction in their cost of living. This can all be done in a way which guarantees energy security. It can also be achieved without building new coal-fired power stations. All clean and cleaner energy options should be embraced.

The reason Australia must act on climate change is not because our aggregate emissions are so large. They are not. In fact, they are barely 2 per cent of global GHGs. But if we become free-riders on the global system, other much bigger emitters will use our free-riding as an excuse not to act themselves. A further reason for Australia having its own house in order is that there is, at present, a growing global leadership vacuum on climate change. We have a fundamental national interest in ensuring GHG emissions are contained in order to keep global temperature increases within 1.5 degrees Celsius this century. We are already the driest continent on earth. Extreme drought is becoming more frequent. Mega-fires will become the norm, as will other extreme weather events, consistent with the predictions provided to successive Australian governments by the Commonwealth Scientific and Industrial Research Organisation (CSIRO). The Great Barrier Reef is at a tipping point. The Murray-Darling is under unprecedented pressure. We therefore have no alternative but to contribute to global leadership on climate. Finally, if we fail to act, Australia runs the real risk of having carbon tariffs imposed on its exports by those countries that are acting on climate change. The European Union (EU) is moving towards this position globally—as is the United States under a Democrat administration. As of 2020, apart from those in the EU, and possibly China, no other major economies have been rising to the urgent international challenge of climate change. We in Australia must work as genuine global leaders and activists on climate change and do so in all global fora of which we are members. Given our vulnerabilities, it's in our national interests that we do so. And we have done so before.

We should turn global climate change action into one of the three core agenda items of the G20, the other two being a return to long-term, sustainable, global economic growth, and the management of global financial stability. It's precisely for purposes such as this that we helped create and then secured

Australian membership of the G20 in the first place. We must, therefore, use it. We should use the G20 to work with countries like India and France to create a new Global Solar Enterprise to fund and coordinate global R&D on large-scale solar energy storage—the single greatest 'moonshot' still needed to achieve the long-term delivery of renewable energy to meet the electricity system's future base-load requirements. But none of this can happen in the absence of Australia resolving its domestic inertia on climate change action—and then having a government with sufficient political courage, imagination and fortitude to lead globally. The uncomfortable truth is that, because of domestic political distractions around the world, very few governments are providing such leadership. Time is running out. And in Australia, we will feel the environmental impact first.

There is one further implication arising from climate change for Australia. A number of neighbouring island states in the Pacific are facing the loss of the land under their very feet to coastal inundation, while at the same time staring down increasingly frequent and intense weather events that could make their territory uninhabitable much sooner than we may think. Australia cannot simply sit back and do nothing. In the event the worst happens, the world will look to Australia and New Zealand to step up. For these reasons, Australia should begin easing residential visa access for our Pacific island brothers and sisters, as the World Bank and others have recommended we do. More importantly, we should also support these Pacific islanders to migrate to higher ground within the region if that is their preference, including by working to provide greater support to some of the larger nations in the region to be able to welcome them. But in planning for the worst, we also need to be conscious above all else of the hard-fought sovereignty of many of these Pacific islanders, and that just because their land may disappear, their countries, independence and identity will not. That is why I am now convinced that, rather than offering a compact-style relationship to the region akin to our arrangement with Norfolk Island, it is better to instead offer an unconditional and open hand to the region, including to help with the enforcement of their lucrative fisheries arrangements, and to support other government services as needed. There are already examples of this, including in Nauru. And what this may evolve into over time should be principally left in the hands of the Pacific islanders themselves.

As foreign minister, I prepared a 2012 Cabinet submission on this, just before leaving that office. As a result, it was not considered by the government. This work remains deeply relevant today, although it will only be possible if both Australia and any of the island states concerned wish it to happen. If they don't, then the problem will have to be dealt with in another way. Some have argued that such an approach is defeatist on the question of saving these low-lying states from inundation. It is not. My argument is that we should be active on both fronts: working as hard as we can to protect these islands in their current state, while also making contingency plans if global efforts fail.

Reforming the Australian Social Contract to Improve Economic Equality

Sustainable economic growth has two basic conditionalities: a natural environment that can support it, and a social contract that ensures that society does not fracture as a result of the inequalities that arise from our existing growth model. Over the last seven years, wages and salaries growth has flatlined, while corporate profits as a share of national income have risen significantly. Absolute inequality in Australia, as measured by the nation's 'Gini coefficient', is rising— just as equality of opportunity, particularly through the education system, is falling. If this trend continues, political support for our current economic growth framework will eventually collapse, polarising politics away from the centre-left and the centre-right towards the extremes. This process is already well down the road in Europe and America. It also contains clear warning signs for Australia.

Australia must now redefine its social contract to reduce inequality before the system begins to fracture. This will depend on multiple policy instruments. Future tax reform must benefit low- and middle-income earners, not further advantage those who don't need redress. Child care must make greater workforce participation easier, not harder. So too with paid parental leave. An Australian Jobs and Training Agency must be fully empowered to deal with structural unemployment arising from the great disruption now unfolding across labour markets from the explosion in labour-disrupting technologies.

Payments to the unemployed must be adjusted to maintain human dignity. The National Health and Hospitals Network, first negotiated in 2010, must be revisited with the states and territories, then fully implemented federally, to ensure that our universal health system is financially sustainable for the long term—rather than slowly dying a death of a thousand financial cuts. In education, STEM reform is not only designed to ensure that the economy can perform in the highly competitive global markets of the future. It is also part of a social contract to ensure that working-class and middle-class kids have access to the well-paid jobs of the future, most of which will lie in the digital economy. A reform of housing policy must also respond substantively to declining levels of housing affordability for young Australians.

One further reform of our social contract arises from the declining affordability and accessibility of higher education. The cost of degrees has now become prohibitive for many students, other than the children of the rich. This represents a major assault on equality of opportunity for the future. This must change. Future cost recovery for undergraduate degrees must be properly means-tested so that the spectrum of cost recovery ranges from 10 per cent to 100 per cent depending on parental income. Every young person qualified to attend university must be accommodated without being deterred by financial disincentive. The gap between the total cost of the undergraduate system and the fees recovered should be met in large part by a new National Education Levy to be imposed on Australia's three biggest mining companies. These companies have gotten away with minimal effective tax rates in Australia over many decades, despite exploiting a non-renewable resource that is actually owned by the Australian people and leased by the corporations. None of them have established charitable foundations at any scale. They have simply maximised hundreds of billions in profits for global shareholders. The time has come to have these corporations 'pay it back' to the nation by becoming a strategic source of funding for the future expansion of the Australian university system.

Finally, the Australian social contract should be expanded by ensuring retirement income adequacy for those on low and middle incomes. The superannuation guarantee level should continue rising to 12 per cent, as we originally legislated in 2010.

The current retirement age of sixty-seven may need to be further adjusted to sixty-nine, reflecting the benefits of greater longevity as well as further sustaining the long-term financial affordability of the aged pension and entitlements system. Our national aged-care system is also now ripe for fundamental national review as quality control, financial sustainability and labour shortages emerge as long-term constraints in providing acceptable care to our seniors. Aged-care reform should include former prime minister Paul Keating's proposal for a Higher Education Contribution Scheme–type system whereby advances are made by the government to ensure first-class care, while these are later recouped in part from the estates of these older Australians once they have passed away. All these measures are designed to make Australia a fairer society than the one it has now become.

National Security: Navigating Major Changes in the Global and Regional Order

Until recently, the long-term global ascendancy of democratic capitalism seemed assured. However, an uncertain America, the rise of China, the resilience of Russia, and India's equivocation about its future global role, coupled with the internal challenges facing Western democracies across the board, have created a new and more complex international political reality. If the sun has begun finally to set on Western economic dominance in the world, by this logic, some argue, the same will follow with the declining global appeal of the dominant Western political idea—namely democracy itself. My argument, however, is that despite the multiple challenges democracy is now encountering in its Western heartland, rumours of its death and decline are premature. Asian democracies have come from nothing over the last quarter of a century. There is still enormous power in the essential idea of a free people, freely able to choose their own government, that continues to animate and inspire peoples everywhere.

Nonetheless, when China becomes the world's largest economy, measured by market exchange rates, sometime during the next decade, it will be the first time since George III was on the British throne more than 200 years ago that a non-Western, non-democratic, non-English-speaking state will occupy that dominant position. China's chosen development model accompanying its rise has been a form of authoritarian capitalism driven by a one-party state. The Chinese Communist Party has never accepted the inevitability of its own demise. It has judged that its political and economic model is appropriate for China's domestic circumstances. And further, following the rise of Xi Jinping in 2012, the party doubled down on its level of political and economic control, explicitly rejecting the idea that China is in some form of long-term evolution to become a Singaporean-style, semi-democratic system. Instead, Xi Jinping speaks with growing candour about Marx, Lenin and China's own hierarchical Confucian tradition as his ideological guides for charting the country's national and global future. This spells the end of American and wider Western assumptions that decades of engagement strategy with China would eventually cause Beijing to accept the inherent wisdom of the existing liberal-democratic rules-based order, crafted by America since World War II, and one which China could happily accept and sustain once it eclipsed American power. Instead, China's chosen future development model, and the emerging patterns of its own global engagement, are likely to have major implications for the future shape of the rules-based system, for China's particular role within our own hemisphere, as well as for Australia itself.

Australia therefore needs a deeply realistic understanding of China's worldview under Xi Jinping. Under Xi, China will consolidate its one-party state rather than the reverse. It will prioritise the preservation of national unity, including conforming Hong Kong and increasingly Taiwan to its own domestic image. It will seek to continue to grow its economy with a revised growth model, but one which will be compromised by a continuing determination to preference state-owned enterprises over the growing ascendancy of major private firms. Xi's China will also seek to navigate the constraints of climate change despite China's continued chronic dependency on coal-fired power generation. China will seek to expand its geo-economic and geo-strategic influence across the Eurasian continent to Europe, Africa and the Middle East through its multi-trillion-dollar Belt and Road Initiative—just as it will deploy its economic and foreign policy influence in East Asia to prize regional states away from the US sphere of strategic influence and into its own, while also using its own military modernisation to gradually push the United States out of its current dominant military position in the western Pacific. Elsewhere in the world, China will seek to become the indispensable economic partner of all, and over time work to change the rules, institutions and practices of the current liberal international order in a direction more compatible with China's own indigenous interests and values.

Each of these individual elements of China's emerging worldview has implications for Australia— some positive, some negative, others still to be determined. Australia will need a strong, sophisticated, national China strategy for the future, as we once had in the past. This should be based on five core principles:

- a clear and consistent articulation of the principles of universal human rights as defined in the Universal Declaration of Human Rights of 1948 and the International Covenant on Civil and Political Rights of 1966, both of which have been signed by China and Australia
- clear and consistent support for the Australia, New Zealand, United States Security Treaty (ANZUS) as a force multiplier in Australia's response to external security pressure

- full commitment to an open trade and investment relationship with China, based on the existing Free Trade Agreement between Canberra and Beijing, reciprocal access to each other's markets, and the principles of international trade law under the General Agreement on Tariffs and Trade, and the WTO
- full collaboration with China in the institutions of global governance, in particular the G20, in dealing with global action on climate change, pandemic management, and financial and economic governance
- where points of fundamental disagreement arise between China and Australia, Australia should manage these disagreements through bilateral diplomacy, but reinforced by a common strategy with other major democracies in Asia, Europe and elsewhere, thereby lessening the likelihood of Chinese punitive actions against Australia if we are working in the company of others.

Because China respects strength and is contemptuous of weakness, Australia must be resolute in the defence of its values and national interests. We will need to significantly increase our national defence expenditure over the decades ahead to expand our naval and air capabilities. This should be entrenched in statute as requiring a minimum of 2 per cent of GDP to prevent the inevitable predations of Treasury, which institutionally sees much of defence as a waste. We should deepen the military relationship with the United States because, in the eyes of the wider region, ANZUS represents an Australian force multiplier which enhances our strategic and foreign policy leverage, rather than the reverse. Australia will also need to radically enhance its strategic diplomacy across the Indo-Pacific region, most particularly in the Pacific island countries where the current government has been derelict in its responsibilities, creating a strategic window for China to enter. Australia should seek to join the Association of Southeast Asian Nations (ASEAN), although this will be resisted by various association members to begin with. ASEAN is becoming weaker and more divided over time. Australian membership would add to ASEAN's economic ballast by more than a third. It would also help Australia and Indonesia manage their own long-term bilateral relationship—particularly as Indonesia becomes more powerful—as common members of an important regional institution. Australia should also work to engage with the Biden administration on US membership of the Trans-Pacific Partnership, to enhance regional economic growth between the open economies of the region—Chinese membership should also be considered in the future. Australia should seek to enhance the East Asia Summit (EAS) as an emerging piece of the region's future security architecture. We should maintain the vision of the long-term development of an Asia Pacific Community, based on the evolution of the EAS, in order to provide a forum for open security dialogue, the encouragement of multilateral security cooperation, and, in time, dispute resolution, rather than simply watch the region degenerate into two armed camps—one in Washington and Tokyo, the other in Beijing and possibly Pyongyang. Finally, Australia, as a G20 member country, will also have a responsibility in the years ahead to work intimately with other G20 states like France, Germany, the United Kingdom and Japan to defend the liberal rules-based international order against threats such as that of US dismemberment during the period of the Trump presidency. If we fail in the above, China will increasingly find itself pushing on an open door. All this will require a much-better-resourced Australian foreign service. It will also need an aid program capable of having competitive influence in the wider region, rather than the one now seen as increasingly marginal.

Global and regional instability is also likely to greatly increase the numbers of asylum seekers worldwide. Already there are almost 80 million forcibly displaced people worldwide. The Europeans once thought this was not their problem. Then they thought it was only their problem. The American experience has been much the same. The truth is it is a global problem. Because Australia is the only Western country in the Indo-Pacific region, it will become an even more attractive destination than before. It will become critical, therefore, for Australia to lead the international debate on the reform of the global institutional arrangements underpinning the relevant UN conventions. This must be done multilaterally. It must deal with the economic development needs of potential source countries. It must deal with the immediate humanitarian aid requirements of the neighbouring countries where asylum seekers first flee. It must also deploy the United Nations High Commissioner for Refugees to transit countries to organise proper reception centres, processing arrangements and humane conditions, funded by international agencies, until the status of asylum seekers is determined. Then it must develop an international agreement on global burden-sharing for all potential destination countries, commensurate with national capacity and economic size. It would be on the basis of this agreement that successful applicants would be resettled. It is only through such an approach that order, humanity and secure national borders can be restored for the future.

Managing Global Pandemics

The uncomfortable truth is that Australia should have been better prepared for the COVID-19 global pandemic than it was. Following the SARS crisis of 2003, there was ample warning that pandemics of this nature could radically impact our country. One of the recommendations of the 2020 Summit held in early 2008 was for Australia to develop a detailed national pandemic plan. In government, we did this, conducting a full-scale national pandemic preparedness exercise between the Commonwealth and the states and territories later that year. In 2009, we then faced a global H1N1 (swine flu) epidemic, originating in the United States, carrying to seventy-five countries, and resulting in the deaths of more than half a million people worldwide, 80 per cent of whom were under sixty-five—Australia suffered 35 000 cases and a total of 191 deaths. We managed the health impact of the crisis relatively well and we did not close down the economy. This was doubly difficult as the outbreak occurred six months after the eruption of the GFC. Unfortunately, our national pandemic preparedness exercise was the last such exercise conducted by the Commonwealth. As a result, by the time COVID-19 struck in 2020, Australia was not properly prepared, as evidenced by the confusion we saw in the Morrison government's public health and economic policy response in the first quarter of that year. The Liberals, who had spent the last decade systematically ridiculing the Labor government's 2020 Summit, its recommendations and the very idea of long-term planning for Australia's future, were caught flat-footed. For this, all Australians have paid a very great price. For the future, Australia must be prepared for a rolling series of global pandemics. This will require five sets of measures:

- the full funding of our national scientific research establishment, led by the CSIRO, focused on the full range of zoonotic diseases
- the full funding of our national vaccine-development R&D effort, led by our universities
- a national plan for full national self-reliance in all critical medical goods and supplies, and related supplies, rather than be exposed to the vulnerabilities of global supply chains
- leading international efforts to fund the GAVI Alliance for global vaccine distribution, as well as the proper funding and reform of the WHO as recommended by multiple reports after the H1N1 crisis
- a rolling national economic and public health contingency plan, and integrated national implementation machinery, for dealing with the next pandemic, including the proper preparation of our aged-care sector given the government's demonstrable failure to do so in the coronavirus crisis.

BROADENING THE POLITICAL BASE OF THE AUSTRALIAN LABOR PARTY

Redressing entrenched media bias, demolishing the credibility of what remains of the intellectual and moral integrity of the Liberal Party project, and outlining a bold policy vision for a Big Australia of the future, will all take political courage. The critics will abound with each. But all three must be done if we are to secure long-term, sustainable, progressive government in this country. But one final task to be tackled is the continuing reform of the Australian Labor Party itself. The Labor Party will never again win government if it remains exclusively the political arm of organised labour. The declining rate of unionisation (now only 15 per cent of wage earners), the declining relevance of industrial awards to non-unionised labour, as well as the changing structure of work, mean that the Labor Party must rapidly adapt. That is not code language for disaffiliation from the trade union movement. Nor is it suggesting there should be a weakening of the industrial relations system, including its protections for wages, working conditions, collective bargaining and an independent industrial commission—all of which were put in place by my government under the *Fair Work Act* after the Liberals' assault on decency through Howard's Orwellian Work Choices regime. What it does mean is that, for the Labor Party to secure 50-plus per cent of the two-party preferred vote in the future, and a primary vote north of 40 per cent, it must garner new levels of support from small business, independent contractors and sole traders, most of whom operate outside the traditional industrial relations system. This will require policy changes on taxation and other regulatory imposts on small business in order to encourage the formation of these enterprises. More importantly, it will require the Labor Party to *think* in terms of small business. At present, given the union-dominated factional structure of the ALP which shapes preselections, there are no structural incentives for candidates or members of parliament to identify with small business interests. That does not mean the party is hostile to their interests. It means that much of the party has been indifferent to their interests. Labor must also become the natural party of technology, the digital economy and innovation. Given its inherently young, creative and progressive nature, this sector should be Labor's natural terrain. At present, it is not. This too will require much policy work on taxation, R&D and venture capital. But, as with small business, this new embrace will require a cultural shift by Labor of a type that has long been natural for the US Democrats. Labor has always been close to the country's manufacturers. It must now become even closer to the tech sector across the board.

The Labor Party as a culture and a party must also become more naturally embracing of people of faith. At present, this group is being increasingly recruited in outer-suburban areas and in regional Australia by the conservatives through a clever process of sociali-sation and politicisation. By contrast, faith traditions increasingly see the Labor Party as nurturing a deep, secular hostility to all forms of the Church—Catholic, Protestant, Pentecostal—and even other, non-Christian religious traditions. This need not, and should not, be the case. The Labor Party needs to offer conscience votes for all its members on the so-called 'life questions', including abortion, euthanasia and stem cell research. Many Australians with conserv-ative beliefs about these individual moral questions need to have a home within Labor's ranks, particularly given that the majority of church members are of modest means, have reformist views on climate change, and support many elements of Labor's social justice agenda. Our task is to create a comfortable political home for such believers. According to the 2016 Census, two-thirds of all Australians continue to believe in God.

These three basic changes are critical in order to broaden the party's natural political base. Otherwise, whatever other changes we may bring about in the overall political landscape, we will not be equipped to command an effective electoral majority in the future. Once again, each of these changes will take courage, given that each of them goes against the grain of the unstated, internal sensibilities of much of the Labor Party's culture. Each of them will attract internal criticism from the professional 'position takers' of the party, who see each internal political debate primarily through the lens of individual political leverage and personal career advantage, rather than as the long-term future of our cause. But unless our leaders are able to seize these challenges to our corporate advantage as a political movement, and therefore to enhance the electoral prospects for the party, the unions and the progressive movement overall, we will fail. Preserving the party's institutional status quo because of political nostalgia, or because this is the path of least political resistance, provides no answer to this dilemma.

TOWARDS A NATIONAL VISION FOR OUR FUTURE: A BIG AUSTRALIA

These are my views on the core elements of a vision for our country's future. It's unapologetically a vision for a Big Australia because I do not believe we can safely guarantee the nation's future in this deeply uncertain world unless we become much bigger than we are. Precisely how much bigger will be a matter for detailed research on what we will need for our future national capacity, although a figure of fifty million people should be within our reach for the second half of the century. That would begin to place Australia in the same league as France, the United Kingdom and, in time, Germany. We would need at least that level of economic critical mass to sustain our long-term social expenditure to support our ageing population.

We will also need to plan for contingencies for our national defence needs in a future where we may no longer have the support of our traditional alliances. It would also consolidate our position as a member of the G20 over time as other nations pass Australia in absolute economic size. Detailed urban planning for how we sustain our cities, our infrastructure and our environment on the way through would be mandatory to accommodate this level of growth. But it is doable without choking our cities and without destroying our environment.

However, this is not just a matter of size. I also believe in a big-hearted Australia, where compassion is writ large in the nation's soul, where equality is no longer a lost idea, and where the fair go is never thrown out the back door. Equally, it is an Australia that thinks big about the type of country we could become, about the new industries we can create from our own home-grown innovation, about the solutions to climate change and water scarcity we can pioneer, about how to preserve the peace and prosperity of an increasingly fractured region and world. A Big Australia is also about the size and scope of our national imagination.

This is an Australia big enough and bold enough in its national vision to dream on a wide canvas, rather than simply contenting itself with being a small and provincial place—what Manning Clark once called the 'narrowers and straighteners'. Instead, ours can be a strong Australia, a competitive Australia, an inclusive Australia, a compassionate Australia and a sustainable Australia. Neither conservative, nor neoliberal, nor embracing the blind socialism of the utopians. Ours, indeed, can be a fourth way. It is a vision for an Australian social democracy that is capable of bringing the nation with us as we navigate the difficult challenges and complex world of the future.